.tiny book of.
PECAN FAVORITES

.tiny book of.

PECAN FAVORITES

CLASSIC RECIPES FOR EVERY SEASON

Small Pleasures
· SERIES ·
hm | books™

Small Pleasures
· SERIES ·

hm|books

PRESIDENT/CCO *Brian Hart Hoffman*
VICE PRESIDENT/EDITORIAL *Cindy Smith Cooper*
GROUP CREATIVE DIRECTOR *Deanna Rippy Gardner*
ART DIRECTOR *Lynn Akin Elkins*

EDITORIAL
RECIPE EDITOR *Fran Jensen*
COPY EDITOR *Emma Pitts*
CREATIVE DIRECTOR/PHOTOGRAPHY *Mac Jamieson*
SENIOR PHOTOGRAPHERS *John O'Hagan,*
Marcy Black Simpson
PHOTOGRAPHERS *Jim Bathie, William Dickey,*
Stephanie Welbourne Steele
ASSISTANT PHOTOGRAPHER *Caroline Smith*
SENIOR DIGITAL IMAGING SPECIALIST *Delisa McDaniel*
DIGITAL IMAGING SPECIALIST *Clark Densmore*
STYLISTS *Sidney Bragiel, Lucy Herndon,*
Yukie McLean, Tracey Runnion
FOOD STYLISTS AND RECIPE DEVELOPERS *Melissa Gray,*
Elizabeth Stringer, Kathleen Kanen, Janet Lambert,
Nancy Hughes, Vanessa Rocchio, Jade Sinacori
TEST KITCHEN ASSISTANT *Anita Simpson Spain*

hm
hoffmanmedia

CHAIRMAN OF THE BOARD/CEO *Phyllis Hoffman DePiano*
PRESIDENT/COO *Eric W. Hoffman*
PRESIDENT/CCO *Brian Hart Hoffman*
EXECUTIVE VICE PRESIDENT/CFO *Mary P. Cummings*
EXECUTIVE VICE PRESIDENT/O&M *Greg Baugh*
VICE PRESIDENT/DIGITAL MEDIA *Jon Adamson*
VICE PRESIDENT/EDITORIAL *Cindy Smith Cooper*
VICE PRESIDENT/IMS *Ray Reed*
VICE PRESIDENT/ADMINISTRATION *Lynn Lee Terry*

Hoffman Media
1900 International Park Drive, Suite 50
Birmingham, Alabama 35243
www.hoffmanmedia.com
ISBN # 978-1-940772-44-8
Printed in China

ON THE COVER:
Brown Butter and Pecan Blondies

Perfect Roasted Pecans

Preheat oven to 350°. Place pecans on a rimmed baking sheet; bake until lightly browned and fragrant, 6 to 8 minutes.

.contents.

.introduction.

The nut with a buttery flavor accentuates recipes, whether sprinkled on top, or as an ingredient within.

ANYTIME MY FAMILY and friends discuss our favorite recipes with pecans, we recall our mother's pecan pies or cookies. Who knew that vegetables or breads are delicious with the addition of pecans? And they shine in every menu course—from toasted pecans and pecan breads to vegetables and desserts.

Of course, we all know pecans are super on sweet potatoes or tossed on cakes and salads. But what about within breads, vegetables, salads, and unique recipes like popcorn mixes? This book is divided into savory and sweet chapters to give you a collection of great choices to prepare in your kitchen. With over 75 recipes, you are sure to find new favorites and a few surprises, too. From a bowl, skillet, or cake stand, may you have fun creating recipes that become your new favorites.

— *Cindy*

.inspirations.

From Grove to Table

FROM THE BEAUTIFUL pecan grove or a few trees you depend on each fall to bring joy to your table, this longtime favorite will add dazzle to your desserts, side dishes, and entrées—making recipes tasty and delicious. Chopped, sliced, or left whole, these versatile nuts fit as well into breakfast and dinner as they do snacks and dessert—and everything in between.

TASTE THE FLAVOR Pecans add the perfect hint of nuttiness to everything from fillings for sweet rolls and pies to the crust of salmon and pork loin.

.chapter one.
SAVORY

THE RICH BUTTERY FLAVOR OF PECANS ONLY
ENHANCES THESE RECIPES. FROM FRIED CHICKEN
TO PECAN CORNBREAD—ALL HAVE THAT
FLAVORFUL CRUNCH IN EVERY BITE.

Honey-Brined Pecan Fried Chicken

4 cups water
¼ cup plus 1 tablespoon kosher salt, divided
¼ cup honey
4 pounds chicken drumsticks
3 cups finely chopped pecans
1½ cups all-purpose flour
1 tablespoon ground black pepper
6 large eggs
Canola oil, for frying
Waffles and maple syrup, to serve

In a large bowl, stir together 4 cups water, ¼ cup salt, and honey until salt is dissolved. Add chicken. Cover with plastic wrap, and refrigerate for at least 4 hours or overnight.

Preheat oven to 350°. Spray a wire rack with cooking spray; place rack on a rimmed baking sheet.

In a shallow dish, stir together pecans, flour, pepper, and remaining 1 tablespoon salt. In another shallow dish, whisk eggs until combined.

Remove chicken from brine; discard brine. Dredge chicken in pecan mixture, shaking off excess. Dip in eggs, letting excess drip off. Dredge in pecan mixture, shaking off excess.

In a large Dutch oven, pour oil halfway up sides of pan, and heat over medium-high heat until a deep-fry thermometer registers 350°. Working in batches, fry chicken, turning occasionally, until golden brown on all sides, about 8 minutes. Place chicken on prepared rack.

Bake until a meat thermometer inserted in thickest portion registers 165°, about 10 minutes. Serve with waffles and maple syrup, if desired.

Southern Pecan Chicken Salad

In a large bowl, combine chicken, grapes, pecans, green onion, and bacon.

In another large bowl, combine mayonnaise, sour cream, mustard, thyme, salt, and pepper. Add mayonnaise mixture to chicken mixture, stirring to combine. Cover and refrigerate until ready to serve. Serve on croissants.

MAKES 12 SERVINGS

8 cups chopped cooked chicken
2 cups halved red seedless grapes
1¼ cups toasted chopped pecans
½ cup chopped green onion
10 slices bacon, cooked and crumbled
1½ cups mayonnaise
1 cup sour cream
2 tablespoons Dijon mustard
1 tablespoon chopped fresh thyme
1¼ teaspoons salt
1 teaspoon ground black pepper
Croissants, to serve

Recipe TIP

Select a favorite pasta salad and side of fresh fruit to complement this delicious entrée.

Apple-Pecan Stuffed Pork Loin with Apple Cider Glaze

MAKES 6 TO 8 SERVINGS

4 slices applewood-smoked bacon
1½ cups chopped Gala apple
¾ cup chopped celery
¾ cup chopped onion
3 cloves garlic, minced
1 teaspoon sugar
1½ teaspoons salt, divided
¾ teaspoon ground black pepper, divided
1 cup crumbled cornbread
½ cup toasted chopped pecans
¼ cup chicken broth
2 tablespoons chopped fresh thyme
1 (4-pound) boneless pork loin, trimmed
2 tablespoons olive oil
Apple Cider Glaze (recipe follows)

In a large skillet, cook bacon over medium heat until crisp, 6 to 7 minutes. Remove bacon, and let drain on paper towels, reserving drippings in skillet. Crumble bacon.

Add apple, celery, onion, garlic, sugar, ½ teaspoon salt, and ¼ teaspoon pepper to skillet. Cook until apple and vegetables are tender, 5 to 6 minutes; remove from heat. Add crumbled bacon, cornbread, pecans, broth, and thyme, stirring to combine.

Preheat oven to 475°.

Place pork loin on a clean surface, and cut into one side of meat, leaving a ½-inch border. Continue cutting loin until it can be rolled out into a rectangle.

Place a piece of heavy-duty plastic wrap on top of pork. Using a meat mallet, pound meat to ½-inch thickness.

Spread cornbread stuffing onto pork loin, leaving a 1-inch border. Roll up lengthwise, jelly-roll style, and secure with butcher's twine. Rub outside of stuffed pork loin with oil, and sprinkle with remaining 1 teaspoon salt and remaining ½ teaspoon pepper. Place seam side down in a roasting pan.

Bake for 20 minutes. Reduce oven temperature to 325°. Pour Apple Cider Glaze over pork loin, and loosely cover with foil. Bake, basting periodically, until a meat thermometer registers 150°, 30 to 40 minutes more. Let rest for 10 minutes. Spoon Apple Cider Glaze over pork loin.

APPLE CIDER GLAZE
Makes 1½ cups

- 1 tablespoon olive oil
- 1 tablespoon unsalted butter
- 2 tablespoons chopped fresh thyme
- 2 teaspoons minced garlic
- 1 cup apple cider
- ½ cup firmly packed light brown sugar
- ¼ cup soy sauce
- 2 tablespoons apple cider vinegar
- ½ teaspoon salt
- ¼ teaspoon ground black pepper

In a medium saucepan, heat oil and butter over medium heat until butter is melted. Add thyme and garlic; cook for 1 to 2 minutes.

Add all remaining ingredients, and bring to a simmer. Cook for 5 minutes, stirring frequently.

Peppered Pork Tenderloin with Citrus Pecan Chutney

2 (1-pound) pork tenderloins
¼ cup plus 2 tablespoons olive oil, divided
1 tablespoon ground black pepper
1 teaspoon kosher salt, divided
1 cup apple cider vinegar
1½ teaspoons orange zest, divided
½ cup fresh orange juice
½ cup sugar
½ cup chopped dried pineapple
⅓ cup chopped dried apricots
1 (3-inch) cinnamon stick
½ cup orange marmalade
½ cup chopped toasted pecans
Garnish: toasted pecans

Rub pork with 2 tablespoons oil, and sprinkle with pepper and ½ teaspoon salt. Set aside.

In a medium saucepan, combine vinegar, 1 teaspoon orange zest, orange juice, sugar, pineapple, apricot, cinnamon, and remaining ½ teaspoon salt; bring to a boil over medium-high heat. Reduce heat, and simmer for 10 minutes, stirring occasionally. Remove cinnamon stick with a slotted spoon, and discard. Stir in orange marmalade, pecans, and remaining ½ teaspoon orange zest.

In a large skillet, heat remaining ¼ cup oil over medium-high heat. Cook pork tenderloin until a meat thermometer inserted in thickest portion registers 145°, about 6 minutes per side. Remove from heat; cover and let stand for 10 minutes. Slice, and serve with chutney. Garnish with pecans, if desired.

Molasses-Glazed Shrimp Salad

Preheat oven to 425°. Line a rimmed baking sheet with foil. Place a wire rack on top of foil.

Wrap each shrimp in 1 piece bacon, securing with a wooden pick. Place on prepared rack.

Bake until bacon is cooked through, about 10 minutes. Brush cooked shrimp with molasses. Sprinkle with Cajun seasoning; set aside.

In a small bowl, whisk together oil, lemon juice, salt, and pepper.

In a large bowl, place mixed lettuces. Pour dressing over greens, tossing gently to coat.

To serve, place desired amount of greens on each plate. Sprinkle with blue cheese and pecans. Top with 3 shrimp. Serve immediately.

MAKES 6 SERVINGS

- **18 large fresh shrimp, peeled and deveined (tails left on)**
- **6 slices bacon, cut into thirds**
- **¼ cup unsulphured molasses**
- **1½ teaspoons Cajun seasoning**
- **¼ cup extra-virgin olive oil**
- **2 tablespoons fresh lemon juice**
- **¼ teaspoon salt**
- **½ teaspoon ground black pepper**
- **6 cups mixed lettuces**
- **1 cup crumbled blue cheese**
- **½ cup pecan halves**

Salmon with Bourbon-Pecan Glaze

2 (6-ounce) skinless salmon fillets
¼ teaspoon salt
¼ teaspoon ground black pepper
1 tablespoon olive oil
2 tablespoons unsalted butter, divided
½ cup firmly packed brown sugar
2 tablespoons bourbon
½ cup finely chopped pecans
Rosemary-Scented Couscous (recipe follows) and asparagus, to serve

ROSEMARY-SCENTED COUSCOUS

MAKES 2 SERVINGS

1 cup chicken broth
¾ cup couscous
½ teaspoon lemon zest
¼ teaspoon minced fresh rosemary

Preheat oven to 425°.

Sprinkle salmon with salt and pepper.

In a large ovenproof saucepan, heat oil and 1 tablespoon butter over medium-high heat until melted. Add salmon, and cook until browned, 1 to 2 minutes. Turn, and cook 1 to 2 minutes more.

In a small saucepan, bring brown sugar and bourbon to a boil over medium-high heat. Boil until sugar is dissolved, 2 to 3 minutes. Stir in pecans and remaining 1 tablespoon butter. Spoon pecan mixture over browned salmon fillets.

Bake until fish flakes easily with a fork, 8 to 10 minutes. Serve with Rosemary-Scented Couscous and asparagus, if desired.

ROSEMARY-SCENTED COUSCOUS In a medium saucepan, bring broth to boil over medium-high heat. Stir in couscous; cover and let stand for 10 minutes. Fluff with a fork. Stir in zest and rosemary. Serve immediately.

Southern-Style Brussels Sprouts

In a large Dutch oven, cook bacon over medium heat until crisp. Add garlic, and cook for 1 minute. Remove bacon and garlic using a slotted spoon, and let drain on paper towels. Discard drippings.

Add Brussels sprouts, 1½ cups water, butter, sugar, salt, and pepper to pan. Simmer over medium-high heat, stirring occasionally, until almost all water has evaporated from pan, about 15 minutes.

Add reserved bacon with garlic and pecans. Cook for 2 minutes. Serve immediately.

MAKES 8 SERVINGS

5 slices thick-cut bacon, cut into ½-inch pieces
2 cloves garlic, sliced
3 pounds fresh Brussels sprouts, peeled, stemmed, and halved
1½ cups water
2 tablespoons unsalted butter
1 teaspoon sugar
½ teaspoon kosher salt
⅛ teaspoon ground black pepper
1 cup chopped pecans

Roasted Cauliflower with Pecans

MAKES 6 TO 8 SERVINGS

2 heads cauliflower
¼ cup olive oil, divided
½ teaspoon kosher salt
½ teaspoon ground black pepper
¼ cup unsalted butter
½ cup chopped pecans

Preheat oven to 350°. Spray 2 rimmed baking sheets with cooking spray.

Slice cauliflower vertically into 1-inch-thick slices. Place in a single layer on prepared pans. Drizzle with oil; sprinkle with salt and pepper.

Bake until tender and golden brown, turning once, 40 to 45 minutes.

In a small skillet, melt butter over medium heat. Add pecans; cook, stirring frequently, until toasted, 4 to 5 minutes. Spoon pecans and butter over cauliflower.

Pecan Rice

In a 3-quart saucepan, heat butter and oil over medium heat. Add pecans, and cook until fragrant, 2 to 3 minutes. Remove with a slotted spoon; set aside.

Add onion, and cook for 2 to 3 minutes, stirring constantly. Add sage and rice, and cook for 2 to 3 minutes. Add broth, salt, and pepper. Bring to a boil; cover and reduce heat to medium-low. Cook until liquid is almost absorbed, about 20 minutes. Remove from heat.

Stir in cranberries; cover and let stand for 5 minutes. Stir in pecans. Garnish with parsley, if desired.

MAKES 6 SERVINGS

3 tablespoons butter
3 teaspoons pecan oil
¾ cup pecans
1 medium sweet onion, thinly sliced
1 tablespoon chopped fresh sage
1½ cups brown jasmine rice
1 (32-ounce) carton chicken broth
½ teaspoon kosher salt
¼ teaspoon ground black pepper
1 cup dried cranberries
Garnish: chopped fresh parsley

Entertaining TIP

Pecan oil has a light neutral flavor, and since it has little taste, it won't cover up or mask the flavor of the foods you are cooking. Pecan oil can be refrigerated and will not get cloudy or thicken.

Sage-Roasted Butternut Squash

Preheat oven to 425°. In a large bowl, toss together squash, oil, garlic, sage, thyme, salt, and pepper. Place mixture in a single layer on a jelly-roll pan.

Bake until tender, 20 to 25 minutes, stirring once. Garnish with sage and pecans, if desired.

MAKES 8 SERVINGS

12 cups peeled and chopped butternut squash
¼ cup olive oil
6 cloves garlic, cut in half
2 tablespoons chopped fresh sage
2 teaspoons fresh thyme leaves
1 teaspoon kosher salt
½ teaspoon ground black pepper
Garnish: fresh sage, toasted pecans

Entertaining TIP

Toasting pecans enhances the great nutty flavor. Place halves on a baking sheet that has been lightly sprayed with cooking oil, and bake at 350° until they become aromatic, about 5 minutes. Keep an eye on them since they are easily scorched.

Twice-Baked Sweet Potatoes

Preheat oven to 350°. Line a baking sheet with parchment paper or foil.

Rub sweet potatoes with oil to coat skins. Place on prepared pan.

Bake until tender, 55 to 65 minutes. Let cool until easy to handle.

Cut a thin slice off top of each potato lengthwise, being careful not to damage skins. Using a spoon, scoop out pulp, leaving ⅛-inch-thick shells.

In a medium bowl, combine sweet potato pulp, ½ cup pecans, raisins, brown sugar, butter, and salt; stir well to combine. Spoon mixture into sweet potato shells.

Return filled potatoes to prepared pan. Sprinkle with remaining ¼ cup pecans. Bake for 20 to 25 minutes.

MAKES 4 SERVINGS

4 large sweet potatoes
Vegetable oil
¾ cup chopped pecans, divided
½ cup golden raisins
¼ cup firmly packed dark brown sugar
¼ cup butter, softened
¼ teaspoon salt

Harvest Salad

Makes 6 servings

1 (6-ounce) bag fresh
    spring mix lettuces
1 cup pomegranate arils
2 navel oranges, peeled
    and sectioned
1½ cups thinly shaved
    fennel
1½ cups toasted pecans
1½ cups shaved
    pecorino cheese
½ cup thinly shaved red
    onion
Kosher salt, to taste
Ground black pepper, to
    taste
Dijon Vinaigrette (recipe
    follows)

DIJON VINAIGRETTE
Makes 1 cup

¼ cup white wine
    vinegar
1 tablespoon chopped
    fresh chives
1 tablespoon finely diced
    shallot
½ teaspoon salt
½ teaspoon ground
    black pepper
3 tablespoons Dijon
    mustard
1 tablespoon honey
¾ to 1 cup extra-virgin
    olive oil

In a large bowl, combine lettuces, pomegranate arils, orange sections, fennel, pecans, cheese, and red onion. Season with salt and pepper. Drizzle with desired amount of Dijon Vinaigrette, and gently toss to coat. Serve immediately with remaining Dijon Vinaigrette, if desired.

DIJON VINAIGRETTE In a small bowl, combine vinegar, chives, shallot, salt, and pepper. Let mixture stand for 10 minutes. Add mustard and honey, whisking until smooth. Whisking constantly, slowly drizzle in oil until mixture is combined. Use immediately, or cover and refrigerate for up to 3 days. Bring to room temperature before serving.

Pear Pecan Salad

In a large serving bowl or on a platter, gently toss together romaine lettuce, endive, arugula, pears, and pecans. Serve with Honey-Dijon Dressing.

HONEY-DIJON DRESSING In a medium bowl, whisk together shallot, honey, vinegar, mustard, salt, and pepper. Slowly whisk in oil.

MAKES 8 SERVINGS

1 head romaine lettuce, torn
2 heads endive, torn
4 cups baby arugula
2 red pears, thinly sliced
½ cup pecan halves, toasted
Honey-Dijon Dressing (recipe follows)

HONEY-DIJON DRESSING
MAKES 3/4 CUP

1 medium shallot, finely chopped
3 tablespoons honey
2 tablespoons white balsamic vinegar
1 tablespoon Dijon mustard
½ teaspoon kosher salt
¼ teaspoon ground black pepper
⅓ cup olive oil

Spiced Pecan Cheese Coins

MAKES ABOUT 60

2 cups self-rising flour
½ teaspoon salt
½ teaspoon ground black
    pepper
¼ teaspoon ground red
    pepper
2 cups shredded extra-
    sharp Cheddar cheese,
    room temperature
½ cup unsalted butter,
    softened
½ (8-ounce) package
    cream cheese,
    softened
½ teaspoon
    Worcestershire sauce
½ teaspoon hot sauce
1 egg white
1 tablespoon water
60 pecan halves

In a medium bowl, sift together flour, salt, black pepper, and red pepper. In the work bowl of a food processor, pulse together Cheddar, butter, cream cheese, Worcestershire, and hot sauce until smooth. Add flour mixture, and pulse until very creamy, scraping down sides of bowl several times.

On a lightly floured surface, roll dough into 3 (2-inch-thick) logs. Wrap in parchment paper, securing at ends. Freeze for at least 1 hour.

Preheat oven to 375°. Line rimmed baking sheets with parchment paper.

Remove logs from freezer. Using a sharp knife, cut logs into ¼-inch-thick coins. Place coins on prepared pans.

In a small bowl, whisk together egg white and 1 tablespoon water. Using a pastry brush, lightly coat each coin with egg wash. Press a pecan half into center of each coin.

Bake until lightly browned, 10 to 12 minutes. Let cool completely. Store covered at room temperature for up to 1 week.

Cranberry Brie Wrapped in Phyllo

Trim and discard rind from top of Brie; set cheese aside.

Preheat oven to 350°. Line a large baking sheet with heavy-duty foil.

Place 2 sheets of phyllo on prepared pan, overlapping to make a 14-inch square. (Keep remaining phyllo covered.) Brush phyllo with melted butter. Repeat procedure with remaining phyllo (2 sheets at a time) and melted butter, reserving ¼ cup butter.

Place Brie in center of phyllo. Make shallow indentations in top of Brie with a fork at ½-inch intervals. Pour remaining ¼ cup melted butter over Brie. Spread cranberry sauce over top of Brie. Sprinkle with pecans and brown sugar.

Fold phyllo up over edges of Brie, and crimp edges of phyllo with hands. Fold foil lightly around edges of Brie to hold phyllo in place while baking.

Bake until lightly browned, about 20 minutes. Let cool for 20 minutes. Remove foil. Serve with gingersnaps and apple slices, if desired.

MAKES 8 TO 10 SERVINGS

1 (35.2-ounce) round Brie cheese
12 frozen phyllo pastry sheets, thawed
½ cup unsalted butter, melted
1 cup whole berry cranberry sauce
¼ cup chopped pecans
1 tablespoon firmly packed brown sugar
Gingersnaps and sliced green apple, to serve

Bacon Pecan Cheese Wafers

MAKES 84

1 (1-pound) block sharp
   Cheddar cheese, finely
   grated
1 (1-pound) package bacon,
   cooked and crumbled
1½ cups unsalted butter,
   softened
1 cup finely chopped toasted
   pecans
½ cup finely chopped green
   onion
½ teaspoon ground red
   pepper
4½ cups all-purpose flour

In a large bowl, beat cheese, bacon, butter, pecans, green onion, and red pepper with a mixer at medium speed until combined. Gradually add flour, beating just until combined. Wrap in plastic wrap, and refrigerate for 2 hours.

Preheat oven to 350°. Line baking sheets with parchment paper.

Roll dough into 1-inch balls. Place balls 3 inches apart on prepared pans. Lightly spray a flat-bottomed glass with cooking spray, and dip bottom of glass in flour. Using bottom of glass, flatten each dough ball to ¼-inch thickness.

Bake until lightly browned, about 15 minutes. Let cool on pans for 2 minutes. Remove from pans, and let cool completely on wire racks.

Cheddar Pecan Rounds

In a large bowl, beat butter with a mixer at low speed until creamy. Add cheese, beating to combine. Add flour, salt, and red pepper, beating until combined. Stir in pecans.

On a lightly floured surface, roll dough into 2 (1½-inch-thick) logs. Wrap in plastic wrap, and refrigerate for at least 1 hour or overnight.

Preheat oven to 350°. Line baking sheets with parchment paper.

Using a sharp knife, cut logs into ¼-inch-thick slices. Place on prepared pans. Bake until crisp and golden brown, 15 to 17 minutes. Let cool completely on a wire rack.

MAKES ABOUT 72

½ cup unsalted butter, softened
1 (8-ounce) package shredded sharp Cheddar cheese
1½ cups all-purpose flour
1 teaspoon salt
½ teaspoon ground red pepper
½ cup finely chopped pecans

Goat Cheese Pecan Balls with Jalapeño Pepper Jelly

MAKES ABOUT 36

1 (8-ounce) package
    cream cheese,
    softened
1 (8-ounce) package goat
    cheese, softened
2 tablespoons minced
    fresh chives
1 cup toasted chopped
    pecans
Water crackers
Jalapeño pepper jelly

In a medium bowl, beat cream cheese, goat cheese, and chives with a mixer at medium speed until combined. Roll cheese mixture into ½-inch balls. Roll balls in pecans to coat.

Place 1 pecan ball on each water cracker. Top with about 1 teaspoon pepper jelly.

Feta Cheese Pecan Balls with Strawberry Preserves

MAKES ABOUT 36

1 (8-ounce) package
    cream cheese,
    softened
1 (4-ounce) package
    crumbled feta cheese
2 tablespoons minced
    green onion
1 cup toasted chopped
    pecans
36 buttery round crackers
¾ cup strawberry
    preserves

In a medium bowl, beat cream cheese, feta, and green onion with a mixer at medium speed until combined. Roll cheese mixture into 1-inch balls. Roll balls in pecans to coat. Place 1 pecan ball on each cracker. Top each with about 1 teaspoon strawberry preserves.

Pecan Cornbread

**1 cup plain yellow
  cornmeal**
¾ cup pecan flour
½ cup all-purpose flour
**1 tablespoon baking
  powder**
1½ teaspoons kosher salt
**¼ teaspoon onion
  powder**
**½ cup roughly chopped
  pecans**
**¼ cup roughly chopped
  fresh sage**
**¾ cup unsalted butter,
  melted**
**1 (15-ounce) can cream-
  style corn**
4 large eggs, lightly beaten
¼ cup sugar

Preheat oven to 400°. Place a 9-inch cast-iron skillet in middle rack of oven to preheat.

In a medium bowl, stir together cornmeal, flours, baking powder, salt, and onion powder. Add chopped pecans and sage.

In a large bowl, whisk together melted butter, corn, eggs, and sugar. Add flour mixture to butter mixture, stirring just until combined.

Carefully remove hot skillet from oven. Spray with cooking spray. Pour batter into hot skillet (it should sizzle).

Bake until a wooden pick inserted in center comes out clean, 30 to 35 minutes. Let cool for 10 minutes before serving.

Pecan and Goat Cheese Biscuits

4 cups self-rising flour
1 teaspoon salt
¾ cup cold unsalted
  butter, cubed
1½ cups pecans, chopped
6 ounces crumbled goat
  cheese, chilled
2 teaspoons fresh thyme,
  roughly chopped
1¾ cups whole buttermilk
2 tablespoons unsalted
  butter, melted
Garnish: cane syrup

Preheat oven to 425°. Spray a 12-inch cast-iron skillet with cooking spray.

In a large bowl, combine flour and salt. Using a pastry blender or 2 forks, cut in cold butter until mixture is crumbly. Stir in pecans, goat cheese, and thyme. Add buttermilk, and toss with your hands until a sticky dough forms. Using a 4-tablespoon scoop, drop biscuits into prepared skillet. Brush with melted butter.

Bake until tops are golden, 30 to 35 minutes. (Loosely cover with foil to prevent excess browning, if necessary.) Garnish with cane syrup, if desired.

Spiced Pecans

Preheat oven to 350°. Line a baking sheet with foil.

In a large bowl, stir together pecans and melted butter. Stir in brown sugar and remaining ingredients until combined. Spoon onto prepared pan.

Bake for 8 minutes, stirring halfway through baking. Let cool completely before serving. Store in an airtight container for up to 1 week.

MAKES 4 CUPS

4 cups pecan halves
3 tablespoons unsalted butter, melted
¼ cup firmly packed light brown sugar
1 teaspoon ground ancho chile pepper
¾ teaspoon smoked paprika
½ teaspoon kosher salt

.chapter two.
SWEETS

WITH PECAN HALVES TOPPING CAKES OR STIRRED
INTO COOKIES, THE FLAVOR IS SCRUMPTIOUS.
FROM PECAN PIE CAKE TO PRALINE FRENCH TOAST
THIS INGREDIENT *MAKES* THE DESSERT.

Black Bottom Cranberry-Pecan Pies

1 (14.1-ounce) package refrigerated piecrusts
1 (4-ounce) bar bittersweet chocolate, chopped
2 tablespoons heavy whipping cream
3 large eggs, lightly beaten
1 cup dark corn syrup
2/3 cup sugar
1/4 cup unsalted butter, melted
1 teaspoon vanilla extract
2 cups roughly chopped pecans
1 cup fresh cranberries
Sweetened whipped cream, prepared caramel sauce, to serve

Preheat oven to 350°. Unroll piecrusts, and divide into 6 equal portions. Press into bottom and up sides of 6 (5-inch) cast-iron skillets. Fold edges under, and crimp as desired.

In a small saucepan, cook chocolate and cream over medium heat, stirring frequently, until chocolate is melted and mixture is smooth. Divide chocolate mixture among prepared crusts. Refrigerate for 30 minutes.

In a medium bowl, whisk together eggs, corn syrup, sugar, melted butter, and vanilla until smooth; stir in pecans and cranberries. Pour batter over chocolate mixture in skillets.

Bake until center is set, 30 to 35 minutes. Let cool completely. Serve with whipped cream, and drizzle with caramel, if desired.

Brown Butter and Pecan Blondies

Preheat oven to 350°. Spray 4 (6-inch) cast-iron skillets with cooking spray.

For blondies: In a medium skillet, melt butter over medium heat. Cook, stirring frequently, until butter turns a medium-brown color and has a nutty aroma, about 10 minutes. Remove from heat, and strain through a fine-mesh sieve.

In a large bowl, beat brown butter and brown sugar with a mixer at medium speed until combined, 1 to 2 minutes. Add eggs, one at a time, beating well after each addition. Beat in vanilla.

In a medium bowl, whisk together flour, baking powder, and salt. Gradually add flour mixture to butter mixture, beating just until combined after each addition. Fold in butterscotch morsels and pecans. Divide batter among prepared skillets.

Bake until a wooden pick inserted in center comes out clean, 25 to 27 minutes. Let cool completely.

For topping: In a medium saucepan, bring cane syrup to a boil over medium heat. Boil, stirring frequently, for 1 minute. Remove from heat, and stir in butter until melted. Stir in cream and salt. Let cool completely. Once cool, whisk in confectioners' sugar; stir in pecans. Pour pecan mixture over cooled blondies. Serve with ice cream, and drizzle with cane syrup, if desired.

MAKES 4

Blondies:
¾ cup unsalted butter
1½ cups firmly packed light brown sugar
2 large eggs
1½ teaspoons vanilla extract
1½ cups all-purpose flour
2 teaspoons baking powder
1 teaspoon salt
½ cup butterscotch morsels
1 cup pecans, roughly chopped

Topping:
1 cup cane syrup
¼ cup unsalted butter
¼ cup heavy whipping cream
¼ teaspoon kosher salt
½ cup confectioners' sugar
2 cups pecan halves

Vanilla ice cream, cane syrup, to serve

Upside-Down Monkey Bread

MAKES ABOUT 6 SERVINGS

**Homemade Bread Dough
(recipe follows)**
½ cup unsalted butter
**¾ cup firmly packed light
brown sugar**
3 tablespoons hot coffee
**½ cup plus 2 tablespoons
chopped pecans,
divided**
½ cup granulated sugar
**1 tablespoon ground
cinnamon**

**HOMEMADE BREAD
DOUGH**
**1 cup warm water (105°
to 110°)**
2 tablespoons sugar
**1 (0.25-ounce) package
active dry yeast**
2½ cups all-purpose flour
1½ teaspoons kosher salt
**2 tablespoons unsalted
butter, melted**

Prepare Homemade Bread Dough, and let rise as directed.

Preheat oven to 350°. In a 10-inch cast-iron skillet, melt butter over medium heat. Add brown sugar and coffee; bring to a boil. Cook, stirring frequently, until sugar is dissolved, about 3 minutes. Remove from heat. Sprinkle with ½ cup pecans.

In a large resealable plastic bag, combine granulated sugar and cinnamon. Lightly punch down dough; shape dough into 2-inch balls. Working in batches, place dough balls in plastic bag. Shake until coated with sugar mixture. Arrange dough over butter mixture in skillet. Sprinkle with remaining 2 tablespoons pecans.

Bake until golden brown, about 30 minutes. Let cool for 2 minutes. Invert onto a serving platter or tray. Serve immediately.

HOMEMADE BREAD DOUGH In a medium bowl, stir together 1 cup warm water, sugar, and yeast; let stand until frothy and bubbling, about 5 minutes.

In the bowl of a stand mixer fitted with the paddle attachment, combine flour and salt. With mixer on low speed, add yeast mixture and melted butter, beating just until combined. Switch to the dough hook attachment. Beat at medium speed until dough is smooth and elastic, about 7 minutes.

Spray a large bowl with cooking spray. Place dough in bowl, turning to grease top. Cover and let rise in a warm, draft-free place (75°) until doubled in size, about 1 hour.

Recipe TIP

To save time, prepare the Homemade Bread Dough the night before and let rise, covered, in the refrigerator. Remove from refrigerator about an hour before baking.

Pecan Pie Layer Cake

1½ cups unsalted butter,
   softened
2 cups firmly packed
   brown sugar
1 cup granulated sugar
1 tablespoon vanilla
   extract
5 large eggs
3 cups all-purpose flour
1½ teaspoons baking
   powder
½ teaspoon salt
1½ cups milk
Pecan Pie Filling (recipe
   follows)
Caramel Cream Cheese
   Frosting (recipe
   follows)
Garnish: pecan halves

PECAN PIE FILLING
MAKES ABOUT 2 CUPS

1 cup sugar
⅔ cup dark corn syrup
⅓ cup unsalted butter,
   softened
2 large eggs
1½ cups chopped pecans
1 teaspoon vanilla extract

Preheat oven to 350°. Spray 3 (9-inch) round cake pans with baking spray with flour.

In a large bowl, beat butter, sugars, and vanilla with a mixer at medium speed until fluffy, 3 to 4 minutes, stopping to scrape sides of bowl. Add eggs, one at a time, beating well after each addition.

In a medium bowl, whisk together flour, baking powder, and salt. Gradually add flour mixture to butter mixture alternately with milk, beginning and ending with flour mixture, beating just until combined after each addition. Pour batter into prepared pans.

Bake until a wooden pick inserted in center comes out clean, 20 to 25 minutes. Let cool in pans for 10 minutes. Remove from pans, and let cool completely on wire racks. Spread Pecan Pie Filling between layers. Spread Caramel Cream Cheese Frosting on top and sides of cake. Garnish with pecans, if desired. Cover and refrigerate for up to 5 days.

PECAN PIE FILLING In a medium saucepan, stir together sugar, corn syrup, butter, and eggs. Add pecans and vanilla. Cook over medium heat, stirring constantly, until mixture is thickened and bubbly, about 5 minutes. Let cool completely before using.

CARAMEL CREAM CHEESE FROSTING

MAKES ABOUT 5 CUPS

**2 cups firmly packed
  brown sugar**
**1 cup unsalted butter,
  softened**
¼ cup water
**1 (8-ounce) package cream
  cheese, softened**
**1 tablespoon vanilla
  extract**
**7½ cups confectioners'
  sugar**

**CARAMEL CREAM CHEESE
FROSTING** In a medium
saucepan, cook brown
sugar, butter, and ¼ cup
water over medium heat
until sugar is dissolved,
about 5 minutes. Remove
from heat, and let cool
completely.

In a large bowl, beat brown
sugar mixture, cream
cheese, and vanilla with
a mixer at medium speed
until creamy. Gradually
add confectioners' sugar,
beating until smooth.

Mocha Pecan Cake

½ cup unsalted butter,
  softened
1 cup water
½ cup unsweetened cocoa
  powder
½ cup canola oil
¼ cup instant espresso
  powder
3 cups all-purpose flour
2 cups sugar
½ cup chopped pecans
2 teaspoons kosher salt
1½ teaspoons baking soda
¾ cup whole buttermilk
3 large eggs
2 teaspoons vanilla extract
**Mocha Frosting (recipe
  follows)**
Garnish: chopped pecans

MOCHA FROSTING
MAKES ABOUT 8 CUPS

½ cup warm water
2 tablespoons instant
  espresso powder
2 tablespoons unsweetened
  cocoa powder
1½ cups unsalted butter,
  softened
7 cups confectioners' sugar

Preheat oven to 350°. Spray 3 (9-inch) round cake pans with baking spray with flour.

In a medium saucepan, melt butter over medium heat. Add 1 cup water, cocoa, oil, and espresso powder, stirring until smooth. Cook, stirring frequently, until mixture thickens, about 5 minutes. Remove from heat; set aside.

In a large bowl, whisk together flour, sugar, pecans, salt, and baking soda. In a medium bowl, whisk together buttermilk, eggs, and vanilla. Add buttermilk mixture and butter mixture to flour mixture, stirring until smooth. Divide batter among prepared pans.

Bake until a wooden pick inserted in center comes out clean, about 18 minutes. Let cool in pans for 10 minutes. Remove from pans, and let cool completely on wire racks. Spread Mocha Frosting between layers and on top and sides of cake. Garnish with pecans, if desired.

MOCHA FROSTING In a small bowl, stir together ½ cup warm water, espresso powder, and cocoa until smooth.

In a large bowl, beat butter with a mixer at medium speed until creamy. Gradually add espresso mixture and confectioners' sugar, beating until smooth. Refrigerate until ready to use.

Caramel Coffee Cake

Preheat oven to 350°. Spray a 12- to 15-cup Bundt pan with baking spray with flour.

In a large bowl, beat butter and granulated sugar with a mixer at medium speed until fluffy, 3 to 4 minutes, stopping to scrape sides of bowl. Add eggs, one at a time, beating well after each addition. Add sour cream and vanilla, beating until combined.

In a medium bowl, whisk together flour, baking powder, baking soda, and salt. With mixer on low speed, gradually add flour mixture to butter mixture, beating just until combined. Spoon half of batter into prepared pan.

In a small bowl, combine pecans, brown sugar, and melted butter. Sprinkle half of pecan mixture over batter in pan. Top with remaining batter, and sprinkle with remaining pecan mixture.

Bake until a wooden pick inserted near center comes out clean, 40 to 45 minutes. Let cool in pan for 10 minutes. Remove from pan, and let cool completely on a wire rack. Garnish with confectioners' sugar, if desired. Spoon Caramel Glaze over cake. Cover and refrigerate for up to 3 days.

CARAMEL GLAZE In a large skillet, cook sugar, 1/4 cup water, and corn syrup over medium-high heat, stirring occasionally, until mixture is honey colored. Remove from heat, and whisk in cream until mixture is smooth. Whisk in butter until mixture is smooth. Cover and refrigerate for up to 2 weeks. Let come to room temperature before using.

MAKES 1 (10-INCH) BUNDT CAKE

1 cup butter, softened
1½ cups granulated sugar
3 large eggs
1 (8-ounce) container sour cream
1 teaspoon vanilla extract
2 cups all-purpose flour
1½ teaspoons baking powder
1 teaspoon baking soda
½ teaspoon salt
1 cup chopped pecans
3 tablespoons firmly packed brown sugar
2 tablespoons butter, melted
Garnish: confectioners' sugar
Caramel Glaze (recipe follows)

CARAMEL GLAZE
MAKES 1 CUP

1 cup sugar
¼ cup water
1 tablespoon light corn syrup
½ cup heavy whipping cream
2 tablespoons butter

Caramel-Pecan Sheet Cake

Preheat oven to 325°. Spray a 15x10-inch jelly-roll pan with baking spray with flour.

In a medium saucepan, bring butter and 1 cup water to a boil. In a large bowl, whisk together flour, sugar, baking soda, salt, cinnamon, and ginger. Add hot butter mixture to flour mixture; beat with a mixer at low speed just until moistened. Add sour cream, beating well. Add eggs, one at a time, and vanilla. Pour batter into prepared pan.

Bake until lightly browned and a wooden pick inserted in center comes out clean, 25 to 30 minutes. Let cool on a wire rack for 20 minutes.

Pour hot Caramel Frosting over warm cake, spreading to edges. Sprinkle with pecans. Let cool completely on a wire rack.

CARAMEL FROSTING In a large heavy saucepan, bring butter, brown sugar, and salt to a boil over medium heat, stirring constantly. Remove from heat; slowly stir in sour cream.

Bring mixture just to a boil over medium heat, stirring constantly. Remove from heat.

Gradually add confectioners' sugar and vanilla, beating with a mixer at medium speed until smooth. Use immediately.

Caramel will thicken as it cools.

MAKES 12 SERVINGS

1 cup unsalted butter
1 cup water
2 cups all-purpose flour
2 cups sugar
1 teaspoon baking soda
½ teaspoon salt
¼ teaspoon ground cinnamon
¼ teaspoon ground ginger
½ cup sour cream
2 large eggs
1 teaspoon vanilla extract
Caramel Frosting (recipe follows)
1 cup chopped pecans, toasted

CARAMEL FROSTING
MAKES ABOUT 2 CUPS

½ cup unsalted butter
1 cup firmly packed light brown sugar
½ teaspoon salt
½ cup sour cream
2½ cups confectioners' sugar
½ teaspoon vanilla extract

Pumpkin Gingerbread with Cream Cheese Pecan Icing

½ cup unsalted butter, softened

1¼ cups sugar

1 cup canned pumpkin

½ cup whole milk

¼ cup dark molasses

2 large eggs

1 teaspoon vanilla extract

2½ cups all-purpose flour

2 teaspoons pumpkin pie spice

1½ teaspoons baking soda

1 teaspoon baking powder

1 teaspoon salt

1 teaspoon ground ginger

Cream Cheese Pecan Icing (recipe follows)

CREAM CHEESE PECAN ICING

Makes about 2 cups

1 (8-ounce) package cream cheese, softened

1 cup confectioners' sugar

1 cup chopped pecans, toasted

1 teaspoon vanilla extract

Preheat oven to 350°. Spray a 13x9-inch baking pan with baking spray with flour.

In a large bowl, beat butter and sugar with a mixer at medium speed until fluffy, 3 to 4 minutes, stopping to scrape sides of bowl. Add pumpkin, milk, molasses, eggs, and vanilla, beating to combine.

In a medium bowl, whisk together flour, pumpkin pie spice, baking soda, baking powder, salt, and ginger. Gradually add flour mixture to pumpkin mixture, beating until combined. Spoon batter into prepared pan.

Bake until a wooden pick inserted in center comes out clean, 30 to 35 minutes. Let cool in pan for 10 minutes. Remove from pan, and cut into 12 squares, or using a 2½-inch round cutter, cut into 12 rounds. Spread Cream Cheese Pecan Icing onto gingerbread.

CREAM CHEESE PECAN ICING In a medium bowl, beat cream cheese and confectioners' sugar with a mixer at medium speed until smooth. Add pecans and vanilla, beating until combined.

Pecan Praline Cookies

Line several baking sheets with parchment paper. In a large bowl, beat butter and sugars with a mixer at medium-high speed until fluffy, 3 to 4 minutes, stopping to scrape sides of bowl. Add eggs, one at a time, beating well after each addition. Stir in vanilla.

In a medium bowl, sift together flour, baking powder, and salt. With mixer on low speed, gradually add flour mixture to butter mixture, beating until smooth. Add cream, beating to combine. Shape dough into a disk, and wrap in plastic wrap. Refrigerate for at least 1 hour.

Preheat oven to 350°.

On a lightly floured surface, roll dough to ¼-inch thickness. Using a 2-inch fluted round cutter, cut dough, rerolling scraps only twice.

Bake until edges are lightly browned, about 10 minutes. Let cool on pans for 2 minutes. Remove from pans, and let cool completely on wire racks.

In a small saucepan, cook caramel bits and ¼ cup water over medium heat, whisking frequently, until caramel is melted and mixture is smooth. Let cool to room temperature.

Spread about ½ teaspoon caramel mixture on center of each cookie. Press a praline pecan into caramel. Sprinkle with sea salt, if desired. Place cookies on parchment paper to dry, about 1 hour. Store in an airtight container at room temperature for up to 1 week.

MAKES ABOUT 60

1 cup unsalted butter, softened
⅔ cup granulated sugar
½ cup confectioners' sugar
2 large eggs
2 teaspoons vanilla extract
3 cups all-purpose flour
1 teaspoon baking powder
½ teaspoon salt
3 tablespoons heavy whipping cream
1 (11-ounce) package caramel bits
¼ cup water
60 purchased praline pecans
Sea salt (optional)

Pecan Pie Cheesecake

Crust:
1¾ cups vanilla wafer
    crumbs
¼ cup firmly packed
    brown sugar
⅓ cup unsalted butter,
    melted

Pecan Filling:
1½ cups chopped pecans
1 cup sugar
⅔ cup dark corn syrup
⅓ cup unsalted butter,
    melted
2 large eggs
1 teaspoon vanilla extract

Cheesecake Filling:
3 (8-ounce) packages
    cream cheese,
    softened
1¼ cups firmly packed
    brown sugar
2 tablespoons all-purpose
    flour
4 large eggs
⅔ cup heavy whipping
    cream
1 teaspoon vanilla extract

Preheat oven to 350°.

For crust: In a medium bowl, combine vanilla wafer crumbs and brown sugar. Add melted butter, stirring to combine. Press into bottom and up sides of a 9-inch springform pan. Bake for 6 minutes; let cool. Reduce oven temperature to 325°.

For pecan filling: In a medium saucepan, stir together pecans, sugar, corn syrup, melted butter, eggs, and vanilla. Bring to a boil over medium-high heat. Reduce heat, and simmer, stirring constantly, until thickened, 8 to 10 minutes. Pour into prepared crust.

For cheesecake filling: In a large bowl, beat cream cheese with a mixer at medium speed until creamy. Add brown sugar and flour, beating until fluffy. Add eggs, one at a time, beating well after each addition. Add cream and vanilla, beating to combine. Pour cheesecake filling over pecan filling.

Bake for 1 hour. Turn oven off, and leave cheesecake in oven with door closed for 1 hour. Run a knife around edges of cheesecake to release sides. Let cool completely. Cover and refrigerate for at least 4 hours before serving.

Classic Pecan Pie

Preheat oven to 350°.

On a lightly floured surface, roll dough into a 12-inch circle. Transfer to a 9-inch deep-dish pie plate, pressing into bottom and up sides. Trim excess dough ½ inch beyond edge of plate. Fold edges under, and crimp as desired. Top with a piece of parchment paper, letting ends extend over edges of plate. Add pie weights. Bake for 10 minutes. Carefully remove paper and weights. Let cool completely.

In a large bowl, whisk together brown sugar, corn syrup, and cane syrup. Add melted butter, eggs, vanilla, and salt; whisk until combined. Sprinkle pecans and dates into prepared crust. Pour brown sugar mixture over pecans and dates.

Bake until center is set, 45 minutes to 1 hour, loosely covering with foil for last 20 to 30 minutes of baking to prevent excess browning, if necessary. Let cool completely on a wire rack. Garnish with whipped topping, pecans, and cinnamon, if desired.

MAKES 1 (9-INCH)
DEEP-DISH PIE

½ **(14.1-ounce) package refrigerated piecrusts**
½ **cup firmly packed light brown sugar**
½ **cup light corn syrup**
½ **cup cane syrup**
¼ **cup unsalted butter, melted**
3 **large eggs**
1½ **teaspoons vanilla extract**
½ **teaspoon salt**
2½ **cups pecan halves**
1 **cup chopped pitted dates**
Garnish: whipped topping, chopped pecans, ground cinnamon

Cranberry-Pecan Pie

Crust:
1½ **cups all-purpose flour**
⅓ **cup all-vegetable**
 shortening
½ **teaspoon salt**
4 to 5 **tablespoons ice**
 water

Filling:
¾ **cup firmly packed light**
 brown sugar
½ **cup light corn syrup**
½ **cup dark corn syrup**
¼ **cup unsalted butter,**
 melted
3 **large eggs**
1½ **teaspoons vanilla**
 extract
1 **teaspoon orange zest**
¼ **teaspoon salt**
2 **cups pecan halves**
1½ **cups dried cranberries**

For crust: In the work bowl of a food processor, combine flour, shortening, and salt; pulse until mixture is crumbly. With processor running, pour ice water through food chute, 1 tablespoon at a time, until mixture forms a ball. Turn out dough, and shape into a disk. Wrap in plastic wrap, and refrigerate for 1 hour.

Preheat oven to 350°.

On a lightly floured surface, roll dough into a 12-inch circle. Transfer to a 9-inch deep-dish pie plate, pressing into bottom and up sides. Trim excess dough ½ inch beyond edge of plate. Fold edges under, and crimp as desired. Top with a piece of parchment paper, letting ends extend over edges of plate. Add pie weights. Bake for 8 minutes. Carefully remove paper and weights. Let cool.

For filling: In a large bowl, whisk together brown sugar and corn syrups. Add melted butter, eggs, vanilla, zest, and salt; whisk until combined. Sprinkle pecans and cranberries in prepared crust. Spoon brown sugar mixture over pecans and cranberries.

Bake until set, 1 hour to 1 hour and 10 minutes, covering loosely with foil during last 10 minutes of baking to prevent excess browning, if necessary. Let cool completely.

Pecan-Date Pie

Preheat oven to 350°.

On a lightly floured surface, roll dough into a 12-inch circle. Transfer to a 9-inch deep-dish pie plate, pressing into bottom and up sides. Trim excess dough ½ inch beyond edge of plate. Fold edges under, and crimp as desired. Top with a piece of parchment paper, letting ends extend over edges of plate. Add pie weights. Bake for 8 minutes. Carefully remove paper and weights. Let cool.

In a large bowl, whisk together brown sugar and corn syrups. Add melted butter, eggs, vanilla, and salt; whisk until combined. Sprinkle pecans and dates in prepared crust. Spoon brown sugar mixture on top of pecans.

Bake until set, about 1 hour, loosely covering with foil during last 30 minutes of baking to prevent excess browning, if necessary. Let cool completely.

MAKES 1 (9-INCH)
DEEP-DISH PIE

½ **(14.1-ounce) package refrigerated piecrusts**
¾ **cup firmly packed light brown sugar**
½ **cup light corn syrup**
½ **cup dark corn syrup**
¼ **cup unsalted butter, melted**
3 large eggs
1½ **teaspoons vanilla extract**
¼ **teaspoon salt**
2½ **cups pecan halves**
1 cup chopped dates

German Chocolate Pecan Pie

MAKES 1 (9-INCH)
DEEP-DISH PIE

Crust:
1½ cups all-purpose flour
⅓ cup all-vegetable shortening
½ teaspoon salt
4 tablespoons ice water

Filling:
1 cup firmly packed light brown sugar
½ cup light corn syrup
½ cup dark corn syrup
½ cup unsalted butter, melted
3 large eggs
1½ teaspoons vanilla extract
¼ teaspoon salt
2 cups pecan halves
¾ cup semisweet chocolate morsels
1½ cups sweetened flaked coconut
Garnish: whipped cream, chocolate curls, chopped pecans

For crust: In the work bowl of a food processor, place flour, shortening, and salt; pulse until mixture is crumbly. With processor running, pour ice water through food chute, 1 tablespoon at a time, until mixture forms a ball. Turn out dough, and shape into a disk. Wrap in plastic wrap, and refrigerate for 1 hour.

Preheat oven to 350°.

On a lightly floured surface, roll dough into a 12-inch circle. Transfer to a 9-inch deep-dish pie plate, pressing into bottom and up sides. Trim excess dough ½ inch beyond edge of plate. Fold edges under, and crimp as desired. Top with a piece of parchment paper, letting ends extend over edges of plate. Add pie weights. Bake for 8 minutes. Carefully remove paper and weights. Let cool.

For filling: In a large bowl, whisk together brown sugar and corn syrups. Add melted butter, eggs, vanilla, and salt; whisk until combined. Stir in pecans. Sprinkle chocolate morsels into prepared crust. Sprinkle coconut on top of chocolate morsels. Spoon brown sugar mixture on top of coconut.

Bake until set, about 1 hour, loosely covering with foil during last 10 minutes of baking to prevent excess browning, if necessary. Let cool completely. Garnish with whipped cream, chocolate curls, and pecans, if desired.

Kentucky Bourbon Chocolate Pecan Pie

MAKES 1 (9-INCH) PIE

- 1¼ cups bittersweet chocolate morsels
- 1¼ cups toasted pecans, chopped
- Buttermilk Piecrust (recipe follows)
- ⅔ cup firmly packed dark brown sugar
- 2 teaspoons all-purpose flour
- ½ teaspoon kosher salt
- 1 cup dark corn syrup
- ⅓ cup unsalted butter, melted
- 4 tablespoons bourbon, divided
- 3 large eggs
- Vanilla ice cream, to serve

BUTTERMILK PIECRUST
MAKES 1 (9-INCH) PIECRUST

- 1¼ cups all-purpose flour
- 1 teaspoon kosher salt
- 1 teaspoon sugar
- ½ cup cold unsalted butter, cubed
- 3 to 4 tablespoons whole buttermilk, chilled

Preheat oven to 375°.

Sprinkle chocolate morsels and pecans into bottom of prepared Buttermilk Piecrust.

In a large bowl, whisk together brown sugar, flour, and salt. Add corn syrup, 3 tablespoons bourbon, melted butter, and eggs; whisk until smooth. Pour bourbon mixture over chocolate and pecans. Loosely cover edges of crust with foil.

Bake for 30 minutes. Uncover and bake until set, about 15 minutes more, loosely covering filling with foil to prevent excess browning, if necessary. Let cool completely on a wire rack. Refrigerate until firm, about 6 hours. Brush with remaining 1 tablespoon bourbon, if desired. Serve with ice cream.

BUTTERMILK PIECRUST In a medium bowl, stir together flour, salt, and sugar. Using a pastry blender, cut in cold butter until mixture is crumbly. Add buttermilk, 1 tablespoon at a time, stirring until a dough forms.

Turn out dough onto a lightly floured surface, and shape into a disk. Wrap tightly in plastic wrap, and refrigerate for at least 30 minutes. Let stand at room temperature until slightly softened, 20 to 30 minutes.

Preheat oven to 425°.

On a lightly floured surface, roll dough into a 12-inch circle. Transfer to a 9-inch pie plate, pressing into bottom and up sides. Trim excess dough ½ inch beyond edge of plate. Fold edges under, and crimp as desired. Top with a piece of parchment paper, letting ends extend over edges of plate. Add pie weights.

Bake until edges of crust are lightly browned, about 10 minutes. Carefully remove paper and weights. Let cool on a wire rack for 30 minutes.

Pecan Chess Pie

- ½ (14.1-ounce) package refrigerated piecrusts
- 1 cup sugar
- 2 tablespoons all-purpose flour
- 1 tablespoon plain yellow cornmeal
- ¼ teaspoon salt
- ½ cup unsalted butter, melted and cooled
- ⅓ cup heavy whipping cream
- 4 large eggs, lightly beaten
- 1½ teaspoons vanilla extract
- 3 cups pecan halves

Preheat oven to 350°.

On a lightly floured surface, roll dough into a 10-inch circle. Transfer to a 9-inch pie plate, pressing into bottom and up sides. Fold edges under, and crimp as desired.

In a large bowl, whisk together sugar, flour, cornmeal, and salt. In a medium bowl, whisk together melted butter, cream, eggs, and vanilla. Add butter mixture to sugar mixture, stirring to combine. Sprinkle pecans in prepared crust. Spoon sugar mixture over pecans.

Bake until center is set, 30 to 35 minutes. Let cool on a wire rack.

Apple Praline Pie

Preheat oven to 350°. Line a baking sheet with foil or parchment paper.

Unroll 1 piecrust, and transfer to a 9-inch deep-dish pie plate, pressing into bottom and up sides.

In a large bowl, combine granulated sugar, 2/3 cup pecans, flour, cinnamon, nutmeg, and salt. Add apples, tossing to coat. Pour apple mixture into prepared crust.

Unroll remaining piecrust, and place over apples. Crimp edges of top and bottom crusts together to seal; crimp as desired. Cut 4 vents in top of dough to release steam. Place pie on prepared pan.

Bake until crust is lightly browned and filling is bubbly, about 1 hour.

In small saucepan, bring brown sugar, butter, half-and-half, and remaining 1/3 cup pecans to a boil over medium heat. Cook, stirring constantly, until sugar is dissolved, about 4 minutes. Pour over hot pie. Let cool slightly in pan. Serve warm.

MAKES 1 (9-INCH)
DEEP-DISH PIE

- 1 (14.1-ounce) package refrigerated piecrusts
- 1 cup granulated sugar
- 1 cup chopped pecans, divided
- 1/3 cup all-purpose flour
- 1 teaspoon ground cinnamon
- 1 teaspoon ground nutmeg
- 1/4 teaspoon salt
- 6 medium Granny Smith apples, peeled, cored, and sliced 1/4 inch thick
- 1/4 cup firmly packed dark brown sugar
- 3 tablespoons unsalted butter
- 2 tablespoons half-and-half

Apple Pecan Cobbler

½ cup unsalted butter, melted
8 cups sliced Granny Smith
    apples (about 4 apples)
3 tablespoons fresh lemon
    juice
1 cup firmly packed light
    brown sugar
1½ teaspoons ground
    cinnamon
½ teaspoon ground nutmeg
2 cups self-rising flour
2 cups milk
1½ cups granulated sugar
½ cup chopped pecans
Vanilla ice cream, to serve

Preheat oven to 350°. Pour melted butter into a 13x9-inch baking dish.

In a large bowl, combine apples and lemon juice; toss gently to coat. In a small bowl, combine brown sugar, cinnamon, and nutmeg. Add brown sugar mixture to apples; toss gently to coat.

In a medium bowl, whisk together flour, milk, and granulated sugar until smooth. Pour flour mixture over melted butter. Top with apple mixture.

Bake for 35 minutes. Top with pecans, and bake until lightly browned, 5 to 10 minutes more. Serve with vanilla ice cream, if desired.

Chocolate Chess Bars with Pecan Shortbread Crust

Preheat oven to 350°. Spray a 13x9-inch baking pan with baking spray with flour.

For crust: In a large bowl, beat butter and brown sugar with a mixer at medium-high speed until creamy, 3 to 4 minutes, stopping to scrape sides of bowl. Add egg, beating until combined. Add flour, pecans, salt, and vanilla, beating until combined. Firmly press dough into bottom of prepared pan.

Bake until crust is light golden brown, about 15 minutes. Let cool completely.

For filling: In a large bowl, whisk together sugar, melted butter, vanilla, cocoa, salt, and eggs until smooth. Pour batter into prepared crust.

Bake until center is set, 35 to 40 minutes. Let cool completely before slicing. Garnish with whipped cream and pecans, if desired.

MAKES 12 SERVINGS

Crust:
1 cup unsalted butter, softened
⅓ cup firmly packed light brown sugar
1 large egg
2¼ cups all-purpose flour
1 cup pecans, finely chopped
1 teaspoon kosher salt
1 teaspoon vanilla extract

Filling:
2 cups sugar
⅓ cup unsalted butter, melted and cooled
2 teaspoons vanilla extract
¼ teaspoon unsweetened cocoa powder
⅛ teaspoon kosher salt
3 large eggs

Garnish: whipped cream, chopped pecans

Pecan Chocolate Tarts

Makes 2 (4x1-inch) tarts

1 large egg, lightly beaten
⅓ cup firmly packed light
    brown sugar
2 tablespoons granulated
    sugar
2 tablespoons unsalted
    butter, melted
2 teaspoons all-purpose flour
1 teaspoon vanilla extract
½ (14.1-ounce) package
    refrigerated piecrusts
⅓ cup lightly toasted pecans
¼ cup milk chocolate
    morsels
Caramel Sauce (recipe
    follows)
Vanilla ice cream, to serve

CARAMEL SAUCE
Makes about 2/3 cup

⅓ cup sugar
⅓ cup heavy whipping cream
2 tablespoons unsalted
    butter
1 teaspoon vanilla extract

Preheat oven to 350°.

In a small bowl, whisk together egg, sugars, melted butter, flour, and vanilla.

Line 2 (4x1-inch) tart pans with piecrust. Divide pecans and chocolate morsels between each. Divide egg mixture between each. Place tarts on a jelly-roll pan.

Bake for 25 minutes. Let cool completely. Serve with Caramel Sauce and vanilla ice cream, if desired.

CARAMEL SAUCE In a small saucepan, cook sugar over medium heat until melted and golden brown (do not stir). Remove from heat, and stir in cream. Return to heat, and cook until sugar is dissolved. Remove from heat, and stir in butter and vanilla. Let cool.

Pecan-Chipotle Tassies in Cornmeal Crust

For crust: In a large bowl, beat butter and cream cheese with a mixer at medium speed until smooth. Reduce mixer speed to low. Gradually add flour, cornmeal, sugar, salt, and chile pepper, beating until a firm dough forms. Turn out dough, and shape into a disk. Wrap in plastic wrap, and refrigerate for 30 minutes.

Preheat oven to 350°. Spray 24 mini muffin cups with baking spray with flour.

Using floured hands, shape dough into 24 balls. Place one ball in each prepared muffin cup, pressing into bottom and up sides.

For filling: In a small bowl, stir together pecans, brown sugar, melted butter, corn syrup, vanilla, chile pepper, salt, and egg. Spoon about 1 teaspoon pecan mixture into each pastry shell. (Be careful not to overfill.)

Bake until filling is set and crust is lightly browned, about 20 minutes. Let cool in pans for 5 minutes. Run a knife around edges of crust, and gently remove tassies from muffin cups. Let cool completely on a wire rack.

MAKES 24

Crust:
- ½ cup unsalted butter, softened
- ½ (8-ounce) package cream cheese, softened
- 1 cup all-purpose flour
- ¼ cup plain yellow cornmeal
- ½ teaspoon sugar
- ¼ teaspoon salt
- ¼ teaspoon ground chipotle chile pepper

Filling:
- ⅔ cup chopped pecans
- ½ cup firmly packed dark brown sugar
- 1 tablespoon unsalted butter, melted
- 1 tablespoon light corn syrup
- 1 teaspoon vanilla extract
- ¼ teaspoon ground chipotle chile pepper
- ⅛ teaspoon salt
- 1 large egg, lightly beaten

Double Chocolate Pecan Tassies

Makes 48

Chocolate Tassie Dough
  (recipe follows)
¾ **cup light corn syrup**
½ **cup granulated sugar**
½ **cup firmly packed brown**
  sugar
4 **large eggs**
3 **tablespoons unsalted butter,**
  melted
¼ **teaspoon salt**
1½ **cups finely chopped pecans**
1 **cup bittersweet chocolate**
  morsels

CHOCOLATE TASSIE DOUGH
Makes 48 mini crusts

1 **cup unsalted butter, softened**
1 **(8-ounce) package cream**
  cheese, softened
1¾ **cups all-purpose flour**
½ **cup unsweetened cocoa**
  powder
1 **tablespoon sugar**

Preheat oven to 350°.

Roll Chocolate Tassie Dough into 1-inch balls; press into bottom and up sides of 48 miniature muffin cups.

In a medium bowl, whisk together corn syrup and sugars. Add eggs, melted butter, and salt, whisking until smooth. Stir in pecans and chocolate morsels. Spoon batter into prepared crusts.

Bake until centers are set and golden brown, 15 to 20 minutes. Let cool completely in pans. Run a knife around edges of tassies to release sides, and gently remove from pans. Store in airtight containers for up to 5 days.

CHOCOLATE TASSIE DOUGH In a large bowl, beat butter and cream cheese with a mixer at medium speed until creamy.

In a medium bowl, whisk together flour, cocoa, and sugar. Gradually add flour mixture to butter mixture, beating until combined. Wrap dough in heavy-duty plastic wrap, and refrigerate for at least 1 hour or up to 3 days.

Cinnamon Pecan Croissant Doughnuts

Line a rimmed baking sheet with paper towels, and top with a wire rack.

Unroll crescent rolls, and stack on a lightly floured surface. Roll into a 2-layer rectangle, sealing perforations. Using a 3-inch round cutter, cut out 8 circles. Using a 1/2-inch round cutter, cut centers out of each circle. Reroll dough to 1/4-inch thickness, and cut out more doughnuts until no dough remains.

In a large stockpot, pour oil to a depth of 4 inches, and heat over medium heat until a deep-fry thermometer registers 360°. Carefully add dough, in batches, and fry until browned, about 30 seconds per side. Let drain on prepared rack.

In a small bowl, whisk together confectioners' sugar, milk, and cinnamon. Drizzle doughnuts with icing, and sprinkle with pecans. Serve warm.

MAKES ABOUT 12

2 (8-ounce) cans refrigerated crescent rolls
Canola oil, for frying
1 cup confectioners' sugar
2 tablespoons whole milk
1/2 teaspoon ground cinnamon
1/2 cup toasted chopped pecans

Butterscotch Pecan Biscotti

In a large bowl, beat butter and sugar with a mixer at medium speed until fluffy, 3 to 4 minutes, stopping to scrape sides of bowl. Add egg and egg white, one at a time, beating well after each addition. Beat in caramel extract.

In a medium bowl, whisk together flour, baking powder, and salt. Gradually add flour mixture to butter mixture, beating until combined. Stir in ½ cup butterscotch chips and pecans (dough will be sticky). Cover and refrigerate for 30 minutes.

Preheat oven to 325°. Spray a baking sheet with cooking spray.

On a heavily floured surface, shape dough into a 10x3-inch log; pat to ½-inch thickness.

Bake for 25 to 30 minutes. Let cool on pan for 2 minutes. Remove from pan, and let cool on a wire rack for 10 minutes. Cut log crosswise into 18 (½-inch-thick) slices. Place slices on baking sheet, cut side down. Bake until lightly browned, about 15 minutes more. Let cool completely on a wire rack.

In a small microwave-safe bowl, heat cream and remaining 1 cup butterscotch chips on high in 30-second intervals, stirring between each, until melted and smooth. Drizzle over cooled biscotti.

MAKES 18

- **2 tablespoons unsalted butter**
- **¼ cup plus 2 tablespoons sugar**
- **1 large egg**
- **1 large egg white**
- **1 teaspoon caramel extract**
- **1 cup all-purpose flour**
- **1 teaspoon baking powder**
- **¼ teaspoon salt**
- **1½ cups butterscotch baking chips, divided**
- **½ cup chopped toasted pecans**
- **½ cup heavy whipping cream**

Chocolate Baklava

4½ cups sugar, divided
3 cups water
2 oranges, sliced
10 whole cloves
2 cinnamon sticks
1½ cups honey
4 cups ground pecans
3 cups ground hazelnuts
2 cups ground cashews
½ cup miniature
    semisweet chocolate
    morsels
⅓ cup unsweetened cocoa
    powder
2 teaspoons ground
    cinnamon
2 (16-ounce) packages
    frozen phyllo pastry,
    thawed
4 cups clarified butter,
    melted
Whole cloves
1 (4-ounce) bar
    semisweet
    chocolate, melted

In a medium saucepan, bring 4 cups sugar, 3 cups water, orange slices, cloves, and cinnamon sticks to a boil over medium-high heat. Cook until mixture registers 225° on a candy thermometer. Remove from heat, and stir in honey. Strain syrup, discarding solids. Let cool completely.

In a large bowl, combine pecans, hazelnuts, cashews, chocolate morsels, cocoa, cinnamon, and remaining ½ cup sugar.

Line a 17x12-inch rimmed baking sheet with 1 sheet of phyllo, letting edges extend over sides of pan. Brush with melted clarified butter. Continue lining pan with phyllo, covering bottom of pan only, to make an 8-sheet layer, brushing each sheet with melted butter. Sprinkle ¾ cup nut mixture over top sheet of phyllo. Cover nut layer with 1 sheet of phyllo; brush with melted butter. Repeat procedure with remaining phyllo, melted butter, and nut mixture. Top last layer of nut mixture with 9 sheets of phyllo, brushing each sheet with melted butter.

Preheat oven to 300°.

Cut baklava diagonally into 1-inch diamonds; insert a clove in center of each diamond.

Bake for 1 hour. Let cool completely.

Pour honey mixture slowly over baklava. Let stand, covered, for 2 days before removing from pan. Place baklava into paper cups; drizzle with melted chocolate. Let stand until chocolate is firm. Store, covered, at room temperature for up to 1 week.

Pecan Cheesecake Bars

Preheat oven to 350°.

In a medium bowl, combine flour and ¾ cup brown sugar. Using a pastry blender or 2 forks, cut in butter until mixture is crumbly. Stir in ½ cup pecans. Press mixture into bottom of a 13x9-inch baking pan. Bake for 10 minutes.

In a large bowl, beat cream cheese and granulated sugar with a mixer at medium speed until smooth. Add milk and vanilla, beating until combined. Pour over prepared crust. Bake for 15 minutes. Let cool for 10 minutes.

In a medium bowl, whisk together corn syrup, melted butter, eggs, and remaining ¾ cup brown sugar. Stir in remaining 1 ½ cups pecans. Pour pecan mixture over cream cheese mixture. Bake until center is set, 40 to 45 minutes.

MAKES 24

- **1½ cups all-purpose flour**
- **1½ cups firmly packed light brown sugar, divided**
- **½ cup unsalted butter, softened**
- **2 cups finely chopped pecans, divided**
- **2 (8-ounce) packages cream cheese, softened**
- **½ cup granulated sugar**
- **½ cup whole milk**
- **2 teaspoons vanilla extract**
- **½ cup light corn syrup**
- **⅓ cup unsalted butter, melted**
- **3 large eggs, lightly beaten**

Double-Pecan and Caramel Brownies

MAKES 12 TO 16 SERVINGS

1 cup unsalted butter
2 (12-ounce) packages
semisweet chocolate
morsels, divided
4 large eggs
¾ cup granulated sugar
½ cup firmly packed light
brown sugar
2 tablespoons instant
coffee
1 tablespoon vanilla
extract
¾ cup all-purpose flour
¾ cup pecan flour (see tip
below)
½ teaspoon kosher salt
2½ cups pecan halves,
divided
Caramel Sauce (recipe
on page 98)

Preheat oven to 350°. Spray a 13x9-inch baking dish with baking spray with flour.

In a large microwavable bowl, combine butter and 1 package chocolate morsels. Microwave on high in 30-second intervals, stirring between each, until butter and chocolate are melted and smooth (about 2 minutes total). Let cool for 10 minutes. Whisk in eggs, sugars, coffee, and vanilla. Add flours and salt, stirring until combined.

Pour half of batter into prepared pan. Sprinkle with 1¼ cups pecans and half of remaining chocolate morsels. Spoon remaining batter over morsels. Top with remaining 1¼ cups pecan halves and remaining chocolate morsels.

Bake until set, 25 to 30 minutes. Let cool completely. Drizzle with Caramel Sauce.

Recipe TIP

Made by simply grinding pecans, pecan flour gives these brownies a dense and decadent texture.

Kentucky Derby Pie Bars

Preheat oven to 350°. Line a 13x9-inch baking pan with heavy-duty foil, letting excess extend over sides of pan. Spray with baking spray with flour.

For crust: In a medium bowl, stir together graham cracker crumbs, melted butter, sugar, and egg white. Press crumb mixture into bottom of prepared pan. Bake for 10 minutes; let cool completely.

For filling: In a large bowl, whisk together brown sugar and corn syrups. Add melted butter, eggs, vanilla, and salt; whisk until combined. Stir in pecans and chocolate morsels. Spoon brown sugar mixture into prepared crust.

Bake until center is set, 35 to 40 minutes. Using excess foil as handles, remove from pan, and cut into bars.

MAKES 24

Crust:
3 cups graham cracker crumbs
½ cup unsalted butter, melted
⅓ cup sugar
1 large egg white, lightly beaten

Filling:
1 cup firmly packed light brown sugar
½ cup light corn syrup
½ cup dark corn syrup
¼ cup unsalted butter, melted
3 large eggs
1½ teaspoons vanilla extract
¼ teaspoon salt
2 cups chopped pecans
1 (12-ounce) bag mini semisweet chocolate morsels

Pecan Diamond Bars

Crust:
1 cup unsalted butter,
    softened
⅓ cup sugar
1 teaspoon vanilla
    extract
1 large egg
3 cups all-purpose flour
1 teaspoon kosher salt

Filling:
½ cup unsalted butter
1 cup firmly packed light
    brown sugar
¼ cup granulated sugar
½ cup cane syrup
4 cups pecans, coarsely
    chopped
¼ cup heavy whipping
    cream
1 teaspoon vanilla
    extract
¼ teaspoon kosher salt

Preheat oven to 350°. Line a 13x9-inch baking pan with parchment paper, letting excess extend over sides of pan. Spray with baking spray with flour.

For crust: In a large bowl, beat butter and sugar with a mixer at medium speed until creamy, 3 to 4 minutes, stopping to scrape sides of bowl. Add vanilla and egg, beating until combined. Add flour and salt, beating until combined. Press mixture into bottom of prepared pan. Using a fork, pierce crust several times. Freeze until slightly chilled, about 10 minutes.

Bake until golden brown, about 20 minutes. Let cool completely. Reduce oven temperature to 325°.

For filling: In a medium saucepan, cook butter, sugars, and cane syrup over medium heat until sugar is dissolved. Boil for 1 minute. Add pecans and remaining 3 ingredients; boil until mixture thickens slightly, about 3 minutes. Pour hot filling over cooled crust.

Bake until topping darkens slightly and is bubbly, about 20 minutes. Let cool completely in pan. Using excess parchment as handles, remove from pan, and cut into small diamond-shaped bars.

Recipe TIP

Bars can be made 1 week in advance. Store bars between pieces of parchment paper in an airtight container at room temperature.

Black Bottom Pumpkin Pie Bars

Preheat oven to 350°. Spray a 9x9-inch baking pan with cooking spray. Line pan with parchment paper, letting excess extend over sides of pan; spray pan again.

In a small bowl, stir together graham cracker crumbs and salt. Add melted butter, stirring to combine. Press mixture into bottom of prepared pan.

Bake until light golden brown, about 8 minutes. Sprinkle with chocolate, and bake 2 minutes more. Let cool completely. Refrigerate until set.

In a medium bowl, beat cream cheese and sugar with a mixer at medium-high speed until smooth, about 3 minutes. Add pumpkin, beating to combine. Add eggs, one at a time, beating well after each addition. Add egg yolk, beating well. Add flour, pumpkin pie spice, salt, and vanilla, beating to combine. Pour pumpkin mixture over chocolate layer.

Bake until set, about 55 minutes. Let cool to room temperature.

In a small bowl, combine pecans and caramel topping. Spoon over pumpkin layer. Cover and refrigerate before serving, up to 3 days. Using excess parchment as handles, remove from pan, and cut into bars.

MAKES ABOUT 18

- **2 cups graham cracker crumbs**
- **½ teaspoon salt**
- **½ cup unsalted butter, melted**
- **2 (4-ounce) bars bittersweet chocolate, chopped**
- **2 (8-ounce) packages cream cheese, softened**
- **1 cup sugar**
- **1 (15-ounce) can pumpkin pie mix**
- **2 large eggs**
- **1 large egg yolk**
- **¼ cup all-purpose flour**
- **2 teaspoons pumpkin pie spice**
- **1 teaspoon salt**
- **1 teaspoon vanilla extract**
- **1½ cups pecan halves, toasted**
- **3 tablespoons hot caramel topping**

Pecan Toffee Brownies

<small>MAKES 24</small>

1 cup unsalted butter
1¼ (4-ounce bars)
  unsweetened
  chocolate, chopped
2 cups sugar
5 large eggs
1 teaspoon vanilla extract
2 cups all-purpose flour
½ teaspoon salt
1 cup chopped pecans
½ cup toffee bits

Preheat oven to 350°. Line a 13x9-inch baking pan with heavy-duty foil.

In a small microwave-safe bowl, heat butter and chocolate on high in 30-second intervals, stirring between each, until melted and smooth (about 1 ½ minutes total).

In a large bowl, beat chocolate mixture and sugar with a mixer at medium speed until combined. Add eggs, one at a time, beating well after each addition. Beat in vanilla.

In a medium bowl, sift together flour and salt. Gradually add flour mixture to chocolate mixture, beating just until combined. Spread batter into prepared pan.

Bake for 10 minutes. Sprinkle with pecans and toffee bits. Bake until a wooden pick inserted in center comes out slightly sticky, 20 to 25 minutes more. Let cool completely in pan. Using a serrated knife, cut into 24 squares.

Caramel Orange-Pecan Popcorn

MAKES ABOUT 20 SERVINGS

20 cups air-popped popcorn
2 cups pecan halves
1½ cups firmly packed light brown sugar
¾ cup unsalted butter
½ cup corn syrup
3 tablespoons water
1 teaspoon table salt
¼ cup orange zest
2 teaspoons vanilla extract
½ teaspoon baking soda
1 tablespoon kosher salt

Preheat oven to 250°.

Place popcorn and pecans in a large roasting pan. Set aside.

In a medium saucepan, bring brown sugar, butter, corn syrup, 3 tablespoons water, and salt to a boil over medium heat, stirring occasionally. Cook, without stirring, until mixture registers 260° on a candy thermometer, 8 to 10 minutes. Add zest, vanilla, and baking soda, stirring to combine.

Working quickly, pour sugar mixture over popcorn mixture, stirring until popcorn is evenly coated. Sprinkle with kosher salt, stirring to combine.

Bake for 1 hour, stirring every 15 minutes. Immediately spread popcorn onto parchment paper to let cool. Store in an airtight container.

Salted Caramel Turtles

In a large bowl, combine pecans and melted chocolate, stirring to coat. Drop pecan mixture by rounded tablespoonfuls 2 inches apart onto parchment paper. Let stand until chocolate is set, about 1 hour.

In a large heavy-bottomed Dutch oven, combine sugar, cream, and corn syrup. Cook over medium-high heat, stirring constantly, until mixture registers 240° on a candy thermometer. Remove from heat, and let cool until mixture registers 190° on a candy thermometer. Spoon mixture over top of each pecan cluster, and sprinkle with salt. Let cool completely. Store in an airtight container.

MAKES ABOUT 48

8 cups pecan halves
2 (12-ounce) bags semisweet chocolate morsels, melted
3 cups sugar
2 cups heavy whipping cream
1½ cups light corn syrup
Coarse kosher salt

Pecan Pralines

2 cups granulated sugar
2 cups firmly packed light brown sugar
2 cups heavy whipping cream
3 cups chopped pecans
½ cup unsalted butter, softened

In a large heavy-bottomed Dutch oven, combine sugars and cream. Cook over medium-high heat, stirring constantly, until mixture registers 228° on a candy thermometer. Add pecans and butter; cook, stirring constantly, until mixture registers 240° on a candy thermometer.

Remove from heat, and beat vigorously with a wooden spoon until mixture just begins to thicken and lose its glossy appearance, 3 to 4 minutes. Working quickly, drop by rounded tablespoonfuls 2 inches apart onto parchment paper. Let cool completely. Store in an airtight container.

Recipe TIP

For a holiday gift, prepare Pecan Pralines, and place in cellophane bags. Place in a coffee mug, and add ribbon and a "tea bag" tag.

Candied Spiced Pecans

½ cup unsalted butter
**2 cups firmly packed light
   brown sugar**
**¼ cup heavy whipping
   cream**
**1 teaspoon ground
   cinnamon**
1 teaspoon ground ginger
**¼ teaspoon ground
   nutmeg**
**¼ teaspoon ground
   cloves**
8 cups pecan halves

Preheat oven to 250°. Line a rimmed baking sheet with heavy-duty foil.

In a large Dutch oven, heat butter over medium-low heat until melted. Add brown sugar, cream, cinnamon, ginger, nutmeg, and cloves, stirring to combine. Cook for 5 minutes, stirring constantly. Stir in pecans. Spread pecans in an even layer on prepared pan.

Bake for 30 minutes, stirring every 10 minutes. Let cool completely on pan. Store in an airtight container.

Turtle Lace Cookies

Preheat oven to 375°. Line several baking sheets with parchment paper.

In a large bowl, whisk together flour, sugar, and baking powder. Add coconut and pecans, stirring well. Add melted butter, maple syrup, milk, and vanilla; beat with a mixer at medium speed until combined, about 2 minutes. Scoop dough by ½ teaspoonfuls, and drop at least 4 inches apart onto prepared pans.

Bake until lightly golden, 5 to 7 minutes. Let cool on pans for 3 minutes. Remove from pans, and let cool completely on wire racks.

In a medium microwave-safe bowl, heat chocolate on high in 30-second intervals, stirring between each, until chocolate is melted and smooth. Spread a small amount of melted chocolate in center of each cookie. Place on a baking sheet lined with wax paper. Top each cookie with a pecan half. Let cool completely on a wire rack.

MAKES ABOUT 60

- ½ cup all-purpose flour
- ½ cup sugar
- ¼ teaspoon baking powder
- ½ cup unsweetened flaked coconut
- ¼ cup finely chopped pecans
- ⅓ cup unsalted butter, melted
- 2 tablespoons maple syrup
- 2 tablespoons whole milk
- 2 teaspoons vanilla extract
- 2 (4-ounce) bars bittersweet chocolate, finely chopped
- 60 pecan halves

Snow-Dusted Pecan Butter Cookies

In a large bowl, beat butter and honey with a mixer at medium speed until creamy.

In a medium bowl, stir together flour, pecans, and salt. Gradually add flour mixture to butter mixture, beating until combined. Cover and refrigerate for 30 minutes.

Preheat oven to 300°. Line baking sheets with parchment paper.

Roll dough into 1-inch balls. Place balls 1 inch apart on prepared pans.

Bake until set but not browned, 25 to 30 minutes. Let cool for 5 minutes. Roll in confectioners' sugar. Let cool completely. Roll in confectioners' sugar again.

MAKES ABOUT 36

1 cup unsalted butter, softened
1/3 cup honey, warmed
2 1/2 cups all-purpose flour
1 1/2 cups finely chopped pecans
1/2 teaspoon salt
Confectioners' sugar

recipe index.